THE BIRD ATLAS

Illustrated by Richard Orr
Written by Barbara Taylor

DK

DORLING KINDERSLEY

LONDON • NEW YORK • STUTTGART

CONTENTS

A DORLING KINDERSLEY BOOK

Project Editor Anderley Moore
Art Editor Sheilagh Noble
Designer Heather Blackham
Production Shelagh Gibson
Managing Editor Susan Peach
Managing Art Editor Jacquie Gulliver
US Editor B. Alison Weir

Bird Consultants Michael Chinery MA
Deslie Lawrence

First American Edition, 1993
10 9 8 7 6 5 4 3 2 1

Published in the United States by
Dorling Kindersley, Inc., 232 Madison Avenue
New York, New York 10016

Copyright © 1993
Dorling Kindersley Limited, London

Distributed by Houghton Mifflin Company, Boston.

CIP data is available.
ISBN 1-56458-327-9

Reproduced in Hong Kong by Bright Arts
Printed in Italy by New Interlitho, Milan

How to Use This Atlas

THE BIRD ATLAS IS ARRANGED in order of continent – the Americas, Europe, Africa, Asia, Australasia, and Antarctica. A double-page spread, such as the one on Africa (right), introduces the continent as a whole. This is followed by pages showing the main places where birds live – their habitats – within that continent.

When turning to any page, you can see which continent it is about by looking at the heading in the top left-hand corner; the habitat featured is given in the top right-hand corner. The sample pages below show how the information is presented on the two main types of pages – continental and habitat pages – and explain the maps, symbols, and abbreviations used.

WHERE ON EARTH?

The red shaded area on this globe highlights the location of the habitat featured on the page. For example, the shaded area on this globe shows the position of Central America and the Caribbean within the Americas.

CONTINENTAL PAGES

These pages introduce the continent and give an overview of the climate, landscape, main bird habitats, typical birds, and amazing birds to be found there. A large map shows the size of the continent, its position on the globe, and major geographical features. There is also usually a feature on how the position of the continent has changed over millions of years, as a result of continental drift.

BIRD SYMBOLS

Symbols of each of the birds illustrated on the page show the main areas where each species lives, although some birds live all over the region. By looking at the key, you can identify the birds and then find them on the map.

Length: 12 in
(30 cm)

HOW BIG?

Labels next to each bird tell you how big it is. The length of a bird is measured from the tip of its bill to the end of the tail. Sometimes male and female birds look different from one another and are very different in size. In these cases, measurements for males and females are given separately. In special cases, the wingspan, length of tail feathers or the height of the bird may also be given. For example, on this page you can find out how big a Quetzal is and also discover the length of the male's remarkable tail feathers.

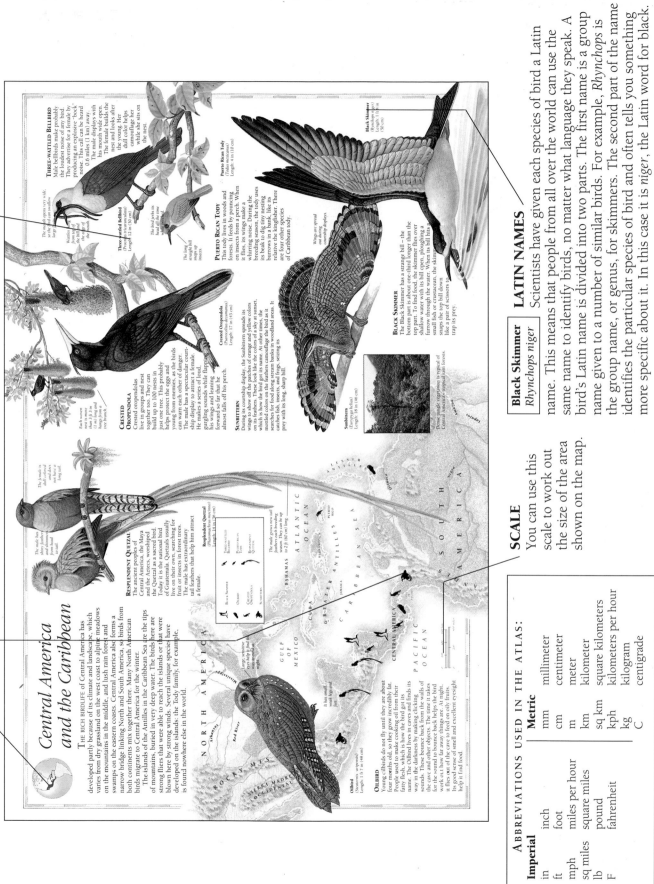

Central America and the Caribbean

THE RICH BIRDLIFE of Central America has developed partly because of its climate and landscape, which varies from dry grassland on the west coast to alpine meadows on the mountains in the middle, and lush rain forest and swamps on the eastern coasts. Central America also forms a narrow bridge linking North and South America, so birds from both continents mix together there. Many North American birds migrate to Central America for the winter.

The islands of the Antilles form the Caribbean Sea in the types of mountains, buried in very deep snow. The birds there are strong fliers that were able to reach the islands or that were blown there by strong winds. Several unique species have developed on the islands: the Tody family, for example, is found nowhere else in the world.

SCALE

You can use this scale to work out the size of the area shown on the map.

LATIN NAMES

Scientists have given each species of bird a Latin name. This means that people from all over the world can use the same name to identify birds, no matter what language they speak. A bird's Latin name is divided into two parts. The first name is a group name given to a number of similar birds. For example, *Rhynchops* is the group name, or genus, for skimmers. The second part of the name identifies the particular species of bird and often tells you something more specific about it. In this case it is *niger*, the Latin word for black.

Black Skimmer
Rhynchops niger

ABBREVIATIONS USED IN THE ATLAS:		
Imperial	**Metric**	
in inch	mm	millimeter
ft foot	cm	centimeter
mph miles per hour	m	meter
sq miles square miles	km	kilometer
lb pound	sq km	square kilometers
F fahrenheit	kph	kilometers per hour
	kg	kilogram
	C	centigrade

What is a Bird?

BIRDS ARE THE ONLY ANIMALS in the world that have feathers. They also lay eggs, breathe air, and keep their body temperature the same all the time. This is called being warm-blooded. Birds developed or evolved from reptiles about 150 million years ago. The earliest bird we know of, *Archaeopteryx* (meaning ancient wing), lived at this time. It was about the size of a crow and had feathers, although it probably couldn't fly very well. From early birds like *Archaeopteryx*, the 9,000 or so species of bird alive today have developed.

Archaeopteryx

Peregrine Falcon
(*Falco peregrinus*)

A bird's wing is light, strong, and flexible, so it will not snap as the bird twists and turns through the air.

A bird uses its tail feathers for steering as it flies through the air.

Birds have scaly legs like those of their reptile ancestors.

The bill is lightweight, but very strong; birds do not have teeth.

BIRD BONES

A bird has a bony skeleton inside its body to support and protect delicate organs, such as its heart, lungs, and brain. But the whole skeleton of flying birds is very light, and the long bones in their wings and legs are hollow, with a honeycomb of stiff supporting struts (above). This means they have less weight to lift off the ground and keep up in the air.

BIRD BILLS

Birds use their bills to catch and hold their food, care for their feathers, and build nests. The size and shape of a bird's bill depend on what it eats and where it finds its food.

Australian Darter
(*Anhinga novaehollandiae*)
Fish-eater

Small Green Barbet
(*Megalaima viridis*)
Fruit and insect-eater

African Paradise Flycatcher
(*Terpsiphone viridis*)
Insect-eater

Pine Grosbeak
(*Pinicola enucleator*)
Seed-eater

EGGS AND CHICKS

All birds lay eggs. The hard eggshell protects the developing chick, and there is a food store inside the egg. Air can pass through the eggshell to reach the developing chick inside. While the chick develops, the parents have to keep the eggs warm by sitting on them. This is called incubation. Many birds are blind, featherless, and helpless when they hatch. Other birds, such as this duckling, stay longer inside the egg, so they are better developed when they hatch. They can run about and fend for themselves almost as soon as they come out of their shell.

A duckling starts to break out of its shell by cutting a circle with its bill.

When the young bird pushes itself out of the shell, its feathers are still wet.

Within three hours its feathers are dry and fluffy, and it can run around.

have powerful chest muscles to help them flap their wings up and down. As a bird flies, this airfoil shape creates an area of low air pressure above it. The high air pressure under the wing and an area of low air pressure under the wing pushes the bird up into the air. Some birds, such as penguins and ostriches, cannot fly; they run or swim very fast instead.

HOW BIRDS FLY

Birds are the largest, fastest, and most powerful flying animals alive. They have a smooth, streamlined shape to cut through the air easily, and their front limbs are wings to push them along, and they

Pigeons and many other birds have a flapping flight. Others, such as eagles and albatrosses, glide long distances without flapping their wings much. Hummingbirds and kestrels can hover.

Rock Dove
(*Columba livia*)

FEATHERS

A bird has a vast number of feathers. Even a small bird, such as a wren, has more than 1,000 feathers. There are three main types of feather — flight feathers on the wings and tail, body feathers to cover the body and give a bird its shape, and fluffy down feathers to keep it warm. Flight feathers are made of strands called barbs that hook together. If the hooks come apart, they can be drawn together again, like zipping up. Each year, a bird sheds or molts most of its old feathers and grows new ones to replace them.

Flight feather from a Guinea Fowl

Body or contour feather from a Red Lory

Down feather from a pigeon

5

Where Birds Live

BIRDS LIVE IN EVERY CORNER OF THE GLOBE. They have spread so far because they can fly from one place to another, live on a variety of foods, and maintain a constant body temperature in most types of weather.

The place in which a bird lives is called its habitat. This is rather like its "home address." A bird's habitat must provide food, shelter, and somewhere to nest. Some birds, such as the Barn Owl, can live in a range of habitats from woodland to scrub; others are more specialized (toucans, for example, live only in the rain forests of Central and South America). Some birds stay permanently in one habitat, while others move away – migrate – at certain times of year. There are an increasing number of human-made habitats, such as houses, parks, and gardens. Some of the most common birds, such as starlings and sparrows, have adapted to live in these new habitats near people.

The main types of bird habitat around the world are shown at the bottom of these pages.

LOOK-ALIKES

Birds have developed in different ways according to the habitat in which they live and the food they eat. The map below shows the world's grasslands and three birds that look similar because they have all adapted to live in similar grassland habitats. This is known as convergent evolution. The ostrich, the emu, and the rhea are probably related, but there are other examples of convergent evolution where the birds are not related at all. For example, the toucans of South America look like the hornbills of Africa and Asia, although they do not belong to the same family.

POLAR AND TUNDRA

The Arctic in the north and the Antarctic in the south are among the harshest environments on Earth. Freezing temperatures, howling gales, and long dark winters mean that few birds can live there, but seabirds nest along the coasts in summer. Surrounding the Arctic is a cold, treeless region called the tundra. In summer, birds such as waders, ducks, and geese flock there to raise their young because of few enemies, plenty of food, and light all the time.

Find out more: pages 8-9, 58-59

CONIFEROUS FOREST

Coniferous trees such as pine, fir, and spruce grow in a huge forest called the taiga, which stretches across the top of North America, Europe, and Asia. The taiga is one of the largest forest areas in the world. Most coniferous trees have needle-like leaves that stay on the trees all year round. Birds feed on the tree cones and help spread the tree seeds. Summers are usually mild, but winters are bitterly cold. Many birds fly south to warmer places in winter.

Find out more: pages 12-13, 28-29

DECIDUOUS WOODLANDS

Deciduous, or broad-leaved, woodlands grow south of the dark conifer woods. Many of the trees, such as oak and beech, lose their leaves in winter, but there is plenty of rainfall all year round, and the climate is generally mild. These woodlands provide plenty of food and nesting places for birds in spring and summer.

Find out more: pages 12-13, 52-53

GRASSLANDS

Grasslands occur where the climate is too dry and the soil is too poor for most trees to survive. Fires are common in this habitat, but the grasses grow back. Grasslands provide plenty of food for seed- and insect-eating birds. Tropical grasslands, such as the African savannah, are hot all year round with long dry spells. Temperate grasslands such as the South American pampas, are cooler, with hot summers and long, cold winters.

Find out more: pages 23, 38-39

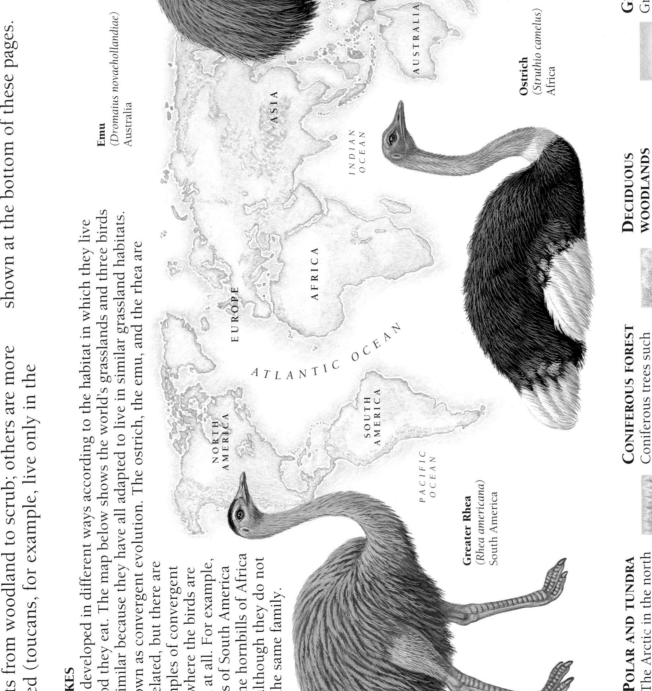

Emu
(*Dromaius novaehollandiae*)
Australia

Ostrich
(*Struthio camelus*)
Africa

Greater Rhea
(*Rhea americana*)
South America

NORTH AMERICA

SOUTH AMERICA

EUROPE

AFRICA

ASIA

AUSTRALIA

ATLANTIC OCEAN

PACIFIC OCEAN

INDIAN OCEAN

ISLAND EVOLUTION

Many rare and unusual birds live on islands, such as the Hawaiian Islands (shown below), the Galápagos Islands, Madagascar, and Japan. These species have developed in unique ways because they have been cut off from their relatives on the mainland for a long time. For example, on the Hawaiian Islands, a finch-like bird arrived some 15-20 million years ago. Since there were few other birds to compete with it, this bird evolved into more than 40 different species called honeycreepers (p.11). Each species found its own type of habitat and food so could live alongside other honeycreepers.

LIVING TOGETHER

In any one habitat, different species of bird live side by side. In a rich habitat, such as a deciduous woodland, various kinds of bird can live on a single tree by feeding and nesting at different levels and eating different types or sizes of food. Some eat insects, while others prefer seeds. In this way, the birds share out the resources of the habitat and are more likely to survive than if they compete with each other for the same things.

Near the top of the tree, tiny birds such as blue tits and wood warblers hang from the smaller twigs and pick insects off the leaves and bark.

In the middle of the tree, birds such as Spotted Flycatchers dart out from a perch to catch flying insects. Woodpeckers chisel into trunks and branches to find insects. They also dig out nesting holes in the trunk.

On the woodland floor, bigger birds such as the woodcock feed and nest. These birds are usually well camouflaged among the dead leaves. Wrens and other small insect-eaters hop nimbly through the dense thickets of leaves and twigs, where they are hidden from enemies.

Wren
(*Troglodytes troglodytes*)

Spotted Flycatcher
(*Muscicapa striata*)

Woodcock
(*Scolopax rusticola*)

Great Spotted Woodpecker
(*Dendrocopus major*)

Blue Tit
(*Parus caeruleus*)

Wood Warbler
(*Phylloscopus sibilatrix*)

MOUNTAIN HABITATS

Mountains such as the Himalayas in Asia (right), the Andes in South America, the Rockies in North America, and the Alps in Europe provide a wide range of bird habitats. The lower slopes have warm forests, but these merge into grasslands and tundra higher up. Above a certain height – called the tree line – there are no trees because it is too cold for them to grow. Near the very top, the ground is covered with snow and ice, and no birds can live there. Mountain birds have to cope with freezing temperatures, fierce winds, and thin air. Some birds move up and down the mountains with the seasons.

SCRUBLANDS

This warm, dry, dusty habitat with tough shrubs and small trees is found mainly around the shores of the Mediterranean Sea, California, and parts of Australia, where it is called the outback or the bush. Many birds move, or migrate, to these scrublands during the long, hot summers, when there are plenty of insects and seeds to feed on. Some fly away for the cooler, wetter winter months.

Find out more: pages 30-31, 52-53

DESERTS

Deserts cover about one-fifth of the Earth's land surface. They are a difficult habitat for birds because there is little rainfall and daytime temperatures are very high. Birds have to rest in the shade during the hottest times of day and either get water from their food or fly long distances to find it. Important deserts of the world include the western deserts of North America, the Sahara, Kalahari, and Namib deserts in Africa, and the Australian deserts.

Find out more: pages 15, 52-53

RAIN FORESTS

Rain forests grow near the Equator where it is hot and wet all year round. They cover less than 10 percent of the Earth's surface but are home to more than half of all the different species of wildlife living on Earth. Many birds live high up in the treetops, where there is more sunlight, warmth, and food. But birds live at all levels in the forest, sharing out the food and space of this rich habitat. The largest birds live on the forest floor.

Find out more: pages 20-21, 36-37, 54-55

WETLANDS

Watery environments are a favorite habitat for birds. Herons, ducks, geese, and swans flock to wetlands because there are plenty of fish, insects, and water plants for them to eat as well as reeds and riverbanks for them to nest in. Trees grow in swampy areas, but there are seldom anytrees on marshland. Drainage and pollution of their wetland habitats by people is a major threat to many of these birds.

Find out more: pages 16-17, 40-41

The Arctic

THE ARCTIC REGION lies right at the top of the world. It is mainly a huge ice-covered ocean, but it also includes the northern edges of North America, Europe, Asia, and Greenland. The ice-free land in the Arctic has a low, flat tundra landscape, with many lichens, mosses, grasses, bushes, and sprawling ground-hugging bushes.

Few birds can live in the Arctic all year round because it is so cold, particularly in winter, when it is also dark all day and all night. During the few light summer months, many birds migrate to the Arctic to nest and feed. At this time of year, microscopic sea plants and animals grow fast in the light and warmth of the sea. They are eaten by fish, which in turn provide food for millions of gulls, auks, and terns. On the tundra lands, some of the ice melts, flowers make seeds, and insects hatch. Waders, ducks, geese, and smaller birds hurry to eat the seeds or insects, lay their eggs, and raise their young before flying south to escape the harsh Arctic winter.

SNOWY OWL

Like a silent white ghost, the Snowy Owl glides over the Arctic tundra, hunting for birds and small mammals, such as lemmings and hares. It will sometimes kill as many as 10 lemmings a day. When there is plenty of food around, these powerful owls lay lots of eggs, so that their chicks have a good chance of survival. When food is scarce, they may not bother to nest at all.

Snowy Owl
(Nyctea scandiaca)
Length: 2 ft 3 in (68 cm)

The female is larger than the male and has more black markings.

Powerful legs and talons attack and carry off heavy prey.

DOVEKIE

These tiny birds look like the penguins of the Antarctic because they live and feed in a similar way. Their bodies are streamlined for swimming underwater and they use their flipper-like wings to push them along. A thick layer of fat under the skin keeps them warm in the cold Arctic seas. Millions of dovekies, or little auks, as they are also called, raise their young on the Arctic coasts in summer. In winter, they move south, but they do not often go far south of the Arctic Circle.

Food is carried in a pouch, or crop. This makes the throat bulge out.

Dovekie
(Alle alle)
Length: 8 in (20 cm)

The male has long tail feathers.

The summer plumage of the male and female is mainly brown with white patches. In winter, it is the opposite way around – mainly white with brown patches.

The female has dark cheek patches.

LAPLAND BUNTING

In the summer months, the Lapland Bunting, or Longspur, migrates to the Arctic tundra to nest. There are no trees in the tundra for it to perch on while it sings to attract females or ward off rival males. Instead, it has to stand on rocks or fly up in the air to sing. It often nests in small groups for protection from predators.

The male's summer breeding plumage helps him attract a female. He becomes much paler than this in winter.

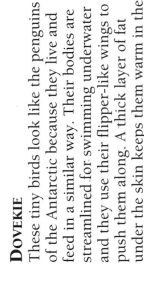

Lapland Bunting
(Calcarius lapponicus)
Length: 6 in (15.5 cm)

LONG-TAILED DUCK

In the Arctic summer, the yodeling courtship call of male long-tailed ducks carries great distances across the open tundra landscape. Some birdwatchers think the call sounds like bagpipes being played. Long-tailed ducks are very good at diving and can plunge as deep as 180 ft (55 m) to chase and catch fish. In shallow water, they take shellfish and other small animals from the muddy bottom.

Long-tailed Duck
(Clangula hyemalis)
Length: 1 ft 7 in (47 cm)

TUNDRA SWAN

These swans, also known as Bewick's swans, nest in the Arctic but migrate long distances to spend the winter in Europe, China, Japan, and the United States. The young swans, called cygnets, migrate with their parents when they are only about three months old. Females lay their eggs in a nest of moss and sedge on marshy ground near water. The nest is usually lined with down feathers, which the female plucks from her breast to keep the eggs warm.

Male and female Tundra swans look exactly the same.

Tundra Swan
(*Cygnus columbianus*)
Length: 4 ft (1.2 m)

Each bird has different yellow markings on its bill.

RED-NECKED PHALAROPE

This is an unusual bird because the female has more brightly colored feathers than the male and takes the lead during courtship. In most other birds, it is the male that looks and behaves this way. The male Red-necked Phalarope also sits on the eggs and takes care of the chicks. They can fend for themselves after about three weeks. When the Arctic winter sets in, red-necked phalaropes migrate south to warmer places. Look for phalaropes spinning like tops on the water.

Red-necked Phalarope
(*Phalaropus lobatus*)
Length: 7 in (18 cm)

A male looks after the chicks, which are striped for camouflage.

ARCTIC TERN

These graceful and elegant fliers travel farther than any other bird and see more hours of daylight each year than any other creature. Arctic terns raise their young during the Arctic summer. When autumn arrives, they fly down to the Antarctic, where summer is just beginning. This involves a round trip of about 22,000 miles (36,000 km) each year. They nest in large colonies and help each other drive away attackers. They dive-bomb enemies such as Arctic foxes or peck at their heads.

A male tern brings his mate a gift of fish during courtship. This food gives the female the extra energy she needs to form eggs.

Arctic Tern
(*Sterna paradisaea*)
Length: 15 in (38 cm)

In the tundra, the ground is always frozen just below the surface. A thin layer of soil above it freezes in winter and melts in summer. Water collects on the surface, forming lakes and swamps where waterbirds can feed.

Map labels

NORTH AMERICA

BEAUFORT SEA

VICTORIA ISLAND

BAFFIN ISLAND

BAFFIN BAY

ELLESMERE ISLAND

GREENLAND

ICELAND

ARCTIC CIRCLE

GREENLAND SEA

EUROPE

SVALBARD

BARENTS SEA

FRANZ JOSEF LAND

KARA SEA

ARCTIC OCEAN
(permanently frozen)

LAPTEV SEA

ASIA

CHUKCHI SEA

SNOWY OWL

LAPLAND BUNTING

ARCTIC TERN

DOVEKIE

LONG-TAILED DUCK

RED-NECKED PHALAROPE

TUNDRA SWAN

The Americas

THE AMERICAS ARE MADE UP of two of the largest continents in the world – North America and South America. North America includes the Caribbean islands and Central America – the narrow strip of mountainous land that links the two continents.

South America is generally warmer than North America and contains the greatest variety of bird species on Earth. It was cut off from the other continents for millions of years and many of its birds, such as the Hoatzin, Oilbird, rheas, and trumpeters, are found nowhere else.

CONTINENTS ON THE MOVE

The Earth's thin surface layer, or crust, is made up of several gigantic pieces called plates, which float on a much thicker layer of liquid rock underneath them. Powerful forces within the Earth move the plates slowly around the globe, carrying the world's great landmasses, or continents, with them. This movement is known as continental drift. The continents of North and South America have not always been in the position they are in today. Over millions of years, continental drift has pulled the two continents apart and pushed them together again, altering their shape and landscape.

About 200 million years ago
all the continents formed one landmass called Pangaea, but this was slowly beginning to break apart.

About 50 million years ago
North America had separated from Europe and Asia, and South America was an island on its own. Many unique and unusual birds evolved in South America because the birds could not mix with those far away on other continents.

About 3 million years ago
the continents had moved into the positions found on our world map today. South America had joined onto North America. Birds could use the Central American land bridge to move north and south between the two continents.

CLIMATE AND LANDSCAPE

The Americas stretch across the whole globe, from the Arctic in the north almost down to Antarctica in the south. All the major habitats in the world can be found there, including dark evergreen forests, sunny broad-leaved woodlands, dry grasslands, humid rain forests, deserts, and swamps. Two huge mountain ranges – the Rockies and the Andes – stretch down the western side of the region and keep birds from moving freely from east to west.

Almost half the world's bird species either breed in the tropical rain forests of South America or visit them on migration. By contrast, North America has no unique species, and its bird life is less varied. One reason for this is the large number of cities and farms in the region, but the colder climate is also important. Less food and shelter are available, and many birds have to migrate to Central and South America during the cold season. Also, the last ice ages wiped out many North American birds or drove them south.

Heavy storms occur in the Caribbean Sea in late summer. They can blow birds off course during their migration from North America.

ROCKY MTS.

NORTH AMERICA

Mississippi

Great Lakes

GULF OF ALASKA

HUDSON BAY

ARCTIC OCEAN

FACTS ABOUT THE AMERICAS

Number of birds
More than 3,100 species of bird live in South America. Colombia alone has more than 1,700 breeding species. Only about 650 species of bird live and breed in North America north of Mexico.

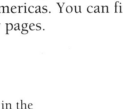

Largest lake
Lake Superior is the largest of the Great Lakes of North America and the largest freshwater lake in the world.

Longest mountains
The Andes are the longest mountain chain on Earth, stretching for more than 4,500 miles (7,250 km) down the western side of South America.

Long river
The Amazon in South America is the second longest river in the world, after the Nile. One-fifth of all the fresh water on Earth flows through it each day. The river pours into the Atlantic Ocean with such force that it is possible to scoop up a glass of fresh water 200 miles (320 km) out to sea.

Highest waterfall
The Angel Falls in Venezuela are the highest in the world at 3,212 ft (979 m).

Highest temperature
Death Valley in North America is one of the hottest places on Earth. Summer temperatures are often higher than 131°F (55°C).

Oldest mountains
The Appalachians are some of the oldest mountains in the world, formed more than 250 million years ago.

Millions of pelicans and other sea birds nest off the west coast of South America. People collect their droppings (guano) for fertilizer.

TYPICAL BIRDS
Here are just a few examples of typical birds from the most important habitats of the Americas. You can find out more about them on the next few pages.

Deserts
All the wrens in the world except for one species live in the Americas. The Cactus Wren prefers a desert habitat.

Mountains
Guans, such as the shy Andean guan, live mainly in the mountain forests of Central and South America.

Woodlands
Crows, magpies, and jays, such as the noisy Blue Jay, are common in the woods of North America. More than 30 species of jay live in the Americas.

Islands
The Akiapolaau is one of more than 40 species of honeycreeper that live only on the Hawaiian islands.

Grasslands
The Burrowing Owl lives on the grasslands and deserts of the Americas. Nearly 60 species of owl live in the Americas, including screech owls and pygmy owls.

Rivers, lakes, and swamps
Perching ducks, such as the Wood Duck, nest in tree holes near water. Other typical ducks of the Americas include whistling ducks, steamer ducks, teal, eider, and scoter.

Rain forests
Nearly 40 species of toucan, toucanet, and aracari live only in American rain forests. The Toco Toucan is a common species.

CARIBBEAN SEA

CENTRAL AMERICA

ANDES

Amazon

PACIFIC OCEAN

SOUTH AMERICA

ANDES

PAMPAS

ATLANTIC OCEAN

Forests and Woodlands

A HUGE EXPANSE OF evergreen forest stretches right across Canada, in a broad belt up to about 500 miles (800 km) wide. It is sometimes called the boreal forest – after Boreas, the Greek god of the North Wind. The cones, buds, and needles of conifer trees, such as pines, spruces, and firs, provide food for a variety of birds, such as grosbeaks, juncos, and crossbills. But the weather is bitterly cold in winter, and many birds fly south to escape the harsh climate.

To the south of these dark forests are areas of woodland where the climate is warmer and moister. The most common trees are broad-leaved species, such as oak, maple, walnut, and hickory, which lose their leaves in winter. The carpet of decaying leaves is full of insects that birds can feed on. There is also a greater variety of nesting places in these sunlit woodlands than in the dark conifer forests farther north.

YELLOW-BELLIED SAPSUCKER

The Yellow-bellied Sapsucker drills neat rows of holes in trees, such as birches, and waits for the sap to ooze out and run down the trunk. Then it laps up the sugary sap with its brushlike tongue. Insects sometimes get trapped in the sticky liquid, and the sapsucker eats these up as well. In winter, the Yellow-bellied Sapsucker migrates south to the warmer climates of Central America and the Caribbean islands.

BALD EAGLE

The national bird of the United States, the Bald Eagle, has a spectacular courtship display. A male and a female lock talons together and somersault through the air. The pair build a gigantic nest called an "eyrie." It is built in a tree or on a rocky cliff and is made of sticks, weeds, and soil. The eagles use the same nest every year and add to it.

The white feathers on its head are fully visible by the time the bird is four years old.

Bald Eagle
(*Haliaeetus leucocephalus*)
Length: 2 ft 8 in (81 cm)
Wingspan: up to 7 ft 2 in (2.2 m)

Fish such as salmon are a common source of food for the eagle.

The maple trees of broad-leaved woodlands turn spectacular shades of red and gold before shedding their leaves in the fall.

If a covey is disturbed, the birds fly off in different directions, to confuse enemies and give the birds time to escape.

NORTHERN BOBWHITE

Outside the breeding season, bobwhites gather in groups of 15 to 30 birds, called coveys. Each covey defends its own special area from other coveys. At night, a covey huddles on the ground in a circle. The birds sit with their heads pointing outward to face danger and their bodies touching to keep warm.

Yellow-bellied Sapsucker
(*Sphyrapicus varius*)
Length: 8 in (20.5 cm)

Northern Bobwhite
(*Colinus virginianus*)
Length: 10 in (25 cm)

The sapsucker presses its tail against the tree trunk to prop itself up.

ARCTIC OCEAN

NORTH AMERICA

ROCKY MTS

PACIFIC OCEAN

GULF OF ALASKA

Great Bear Lake

Great Slave Lake

Rio Grande

750 km
500 miles
500
250
250
0
0

YELLOW-BELLIED SAPSUCKER
NORTHERN CARDINAL
WHIP-POOR-WILL
BALD EAGLE
RUFFED GROUSE
AMERICAN ROBIN
NORTHERN BOBWHITE

OWLS – THE NIGHT HUNTERS

Owls are one of the most characteristic birds of woodland areas. They have short, rounded wings, so they can fly easily between the trees. Most owls are night hunters, using their keen hearing and eyesight to catch food in the dark. They have large eyes and can turn their heads right around to see behind them. Owls collect sounds in their round faces and funnel them toward their feathered flaps of skin on the sides of the face.

Owls have powerful legs with needle-sharp, curved talons for gripping prey.

Light feathers have a soft fringe, to break up the flow of air and muffle the sound of the wings. Owls make very little noise as they fly.

The owl's outer toe can point either forward or backward for extra grip.

The woodland owl swoops silently down from a perch, swinging its feet forward at the last minute to grab its prey. It swallows it whole, but it cannot digest bones, fur, or feathers, so it coughs these up in the form of pellets. You can find these near conifers.

RUFFED GROUSE

In spring, the male Ruffed Grouse often sits on a log and makes a drumming sound by beating his wings to and fro. The sound gets faster and faster, carrying a long way through the forest and helping to attract a female. She nests among aspen trees, feeding on the tree catkins while she sits on her eggs to keep them warm. In winter, the Ruffed Grouse grows comblike bristles on its toes, which act as snowshoes.

During display, neck ruffs extend and tail spreads out like a fan.

The male beats his wings to attract a mate.

Ruffed Grouse
(*Bonasa umbellus*)
Length: 17 in (43 cm)

WHIP-POOR-WILL

During the day, the Whip-poor-will sleeps on the forest floor. Its mottled colors match the dead leaves, so it is hard to see. At night, it flies close to the ground with its mouth open, scooping up flying insects. The bird is so named because of its call, which sounds like "whip-poor-will." It may repeat the call a hundred times or more without stopping.

Whip-poor-will
(*Caprimulgus vociferus*)
Length: 10 in (25 cm)

Mottled feathers ensure that the bird is well camouflaged among dead leaves.

NORTHERN CARDINAL

Cardinals have a rich variety of songs, and males and females, may sing in turn, as if replying to each other. Unlike other birds that live in territories just for the breeding season, cardinals sing all year round to keep other birds away. The cardinal is named after the bright red robes worn by Roman Catholic cardinals.

The male cardinal is far more colorful than the female.

Northern Cardinal
(*Cardinalis cardinalis*)
Length: 9 in (22 cm)

AMERICAN ROBIN

The robin originally nested in open woodlands, but it has adapted well to suburban gardens. It often builds a nest on a house porch or in a nearby tree. It eats insects and worms and also likes fruit, especially in winter. It sometimes spends the winter in northern conifer forests, gathering in large roosts of thousands of birds.

Keen eyesight helps it find worms.

American Robin
(*Turdus migratorius*)
Length: 10 in (25 cm)

Western Mountains

THE WESTERN MOUNTAIN RANGES, such as the Rockies, the Cascade ranges, and the Sierra Nevada, provide a variety of habitats for birds, concentrated in a small space. The warm, wet weather on the lower mountain slopes encourages the growth of dense forests. These forests shelter and feed many birds, from woodpeckers and nutcrackers to jays and chickadees. Higher up the mountains, it is cooler and drier, and the forests give way to grassy meadows and bare, rocky ground on the frozen peaks. Here, eagles and other birds of prey soar aloft on rising air currents, which sweep over the mountains. A few unusual birds, such as ptarmigans, survive on the higher slopes; their downy feathers keep them warm.

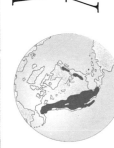

BLACK-BILLED MAGPIE
The Black-billed Magpie is an adaptable bird that eats a range of foods, especially insects and small rodents. It often perches on the backs of cattle and sheep to pick off the ticks and maggots that live on its skin. It builds a large, strong nest of twigs, mud, and plant material lined with fine grass and hair. A dome of sticks, often thorny ones, protects the top of the nest from enemies.

Golden Eagle
(*Aquila chrysaetos*)
Length: up to 3 ft 3 in (1 m)
Wingspan: up to 6 ft 6 in (2 m)

The powerful, hooked bill tears flesh from prey.

GOLDEN EAGLE
To hunt for food, the Golden Eagle soars high up in the sky on its powerful wings. When its sharp eyes spot a small mammal, it dives down quickly to seize its prey and crush it in its hooked talons. The Golden Eagle will attack animals as big as deer, especially in winter. It nests on rocky crags or in tall trees; the nest of sticks can be enormous.

The eagle has strong talons.

Vast areas of coniferous forest at the base of the Rockies shelter less hardy birds from harsh weather.

Black-billed Magpie
(*Pica pica*)
Length: 20 in (50 cm)

The tail is longer than the body.

WHITE-TAILED PTARMIGAN
In winter, this ptarmigan grows white feathers, which camouflage it against the snowy landscape. It often crouches down in the snow to keep out of the fierce, cold mountain winds and avoid enemies. It tends to run away from danger instead of flying. During the summer breeding season, it grows mottled brown feathers. These are very useful to the female, as they hide her while she is sitting on her eggs.

White-tailed Ptarmigan
(*Lagopus leucurus*)
Length: 12 in (32 cm)

Feathered feet keep it warm. Scales on toes act as snowshoes to stop bird from sinking into snow.

Mountain Chickadee
(*Parus gambeli*)
Length: 6 in (15 cm)

MOUNTAIN CHICKADEE
In spring and summer, the Mountain Chickadee nests in the mountain forests, but it moves down to warmer valleys during the cold winter months. There it joins flocks of other small birds, such as warblers and vireos, which move around the valley forests searching for food. If chickadees kept to their own territories in winter, they would not find enough food to eat.

The chickadee feeds on insects and seeds in conifers, such as this Douglas fir.

Deserts

THE HOT, DRY DESERTS of the southwestern United States are home to a surprising variety of birds. To cope with the heat, birds rest in the shade of rocks or inside burrows dug by desert mammals. Long legs also help birds lose heat. There is little water to drink – the Mojave and Sonoran Deserts receive less than 8 in (20 cm) of rain each year and the Great Basin Desert only less than 2 in (5 cm) each year. Birds are forced to get most of the water they need from their food, such as seeds, other animals, and water-filled cacti. The spiny branches of cacti help protect the nests of many birds. It is much cooler inside the cactus, out of the heat of the sun. There are few cacti in the Great Basin Desert, but the many sagebrush bushes are rich in energy-giving fats for birds to eat.

CACTUS WREN

This is the largest North American wren. Like other wrens, it builds several nests – some to shelter in, some to sleep in, and a few for the eggs and young. The nests are dome-shaped with a tunnel-like entrance and are built on a prickly cholla cactus or a spiny yucca or mesquite tree. The spiny branches of cacti help protect the nests of the wren doesn't seem to mind the sharp spines, but enemies find it hard to reach the nest.

Cactus Wren
(*Campylorhynchus brunneicapillus*)
Length: 8 in (21 cm)

ELF OWL

This is the smallest owl in the world – no bigger than an adult's hand. It feeds mainly at night, catching insects with its feet. It will also eat scorpions, taking out the stinger or crushing it before starting to eat. It roosts by day in holes in giant cacti dug by other birds, to escape the heat of the sun. If captured, the Elf Owl pretends to be dead until it thinks the danger has passed.

Elf Owl
Micrathene whitneyi
Length 6 in (14 cm)

GREATER ROADRUNNER

The roadrunner is really a type of cuckoo that lives on the ground. This shy bird is often seen on roads but runs rapidly away from danger and chases anything that moves. On its long, powerful legs, it can sprint at up to 15 mph (24 kph), fluttering its stubby wings for extra speed. Its long tail acts as a brake or rudder to help the bird stop or change direction.

The roadrunner eats lizards, gophers, mice, scorpions, insects, and small rattlesnakes.

Greater Roadrunner
(*Geococcyx californianus*)
Length: 2 ft (61 cm)

PACIFIC OCEAN

GULF OF ALASKA

0   200   400   600 km
0   200   400 miles

NORTH AMERICA

ROCKY MTS

GREAT BASIN

DEATH VALLEY

MOJAVE DESERT

SONORAN DESERT

GULF OF CALIFORNIA

SIERRA MADRE OCCIDENTAL

Rio Grande

ROCKY MTS

GREAT PLAINS

Red River

Arkansas

GULF OF MEXICO

HUDSON BAY

MOUNTAIN CHICKADEE
BLACK-BILLED MAGPIE
GOLDEN EAGLE
ELF OWL
WHITE-TAILED PTARMIGAN
CACTUS WREN
GREATER ROADRUNNER

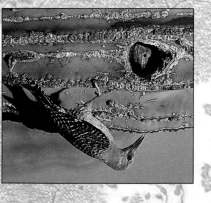

A Gila Woodpecker perches on a giant desert cactus to feed insects to its young nesting inside

The Wetlands

THE RIVERS, LAKES, MARSHES, and swamps of North America, or wetlands as they are known, are a rich habitat for birds because of the variety of food and nesting places they provide. Many marshes were protected so people could hunt the ducks and geese, but they are now wildlife refuges. In the Southeast are swamps dominated by bald cypress trees heaped with vines, Spanish moss, and orchids. These include the bayous of the Mississippi delta and the Florida Everglades. An amazing number of ponds and lakes are scattered over North America. Some formed at the end of the Ice Age, a million years ago, where ice sheets dug hollows in the land. Others formed as a result of movements of the Earth's crust. Many North American wetlands are threatened by the pollution and drainage caused by farms and factories.

Roseate Spoonbill

Belted Kingfisher

Whooping Crane

Green-backed Heron

Anhinga

Common Loon

Snail Kite

Wingtips are jet black.

Head and neck are stretched forward, and feet are straight out behind.

WHOOPING CRANE

The Whooping Crane is one of the world's most endangered species. It almost died out during the 1940s, but its numbers are slowly increasing, thanks to conservation. It nests in northwestern Canada but migrates south to the warmer weather of the Texas coastline in winter. Its name comes from its loud, trumpeting call. Whooping cranes mate for life; they are very attentive parents.

Whooping Crane
(*Grus americana*)
Length: 4 ft 3 in (1.3 m)

Summer

Winter

COMMON LOON

The Common Loon, or diver, as it is sometimes known, plunges up to 266 ft (81 m) below the waters of lakes, rivers, and seas. Its feet are set well back on its body, to push it through the water when it dives. On dry land, its graceful glide turns into a wobbly walk. It has a sad, yodeling call; sometimes it wails and laughs wildly. These calls sound eerie at night.

Common Loon
(*Gavia immer*)
Length: 3 ft (90 cm)

In winter the loon's plumage is much paler and duller than in summer.

Large broad wings help the bird soar.

The Everglades (see map on facing page).

North American lakes, surrounded by coniferous forest, like this one on the northwest coast of Canada, are home to wading birds, such as loons and cranes.

APPALACHIAN MTS

St. Lawrence

Great Lakes

Mississippi

Red

GULF OF MEXICO

Rio Grande

SIERRA MADRE

Colorado

ROCKY MTS

NORTH AMERICA

Great Bear Lake

Great Slave Lake

PACIFIC OCEAN

0   250   500   750 km

0   250   500 miles

Belted Kingfisher
(*Megaceryle alcyon*)
Length: 13 in (33 cm)

You can tell the female by her rusty belly band below the slate blue breast band.

The stout, sharp bill is used to spear fish.

BELTED KINGFISHER

This is the only kingfisher in most of North America. It usually hovers over the water, then plunges in headfirst, to grab a fish in its strong bill. It also swoops close to the water's surface and dips down to catch a meal. It has a loud, rattling call, often made as it flies. The female lays her eggs at the end of a long tunnel in a steep bank near the water.